Mr N

Holiday

Written by Diana Noonan
Illustrated by Paul Könye

Mr Merton liked things to be on time. He used his watch to keep his family on time.

He liked beds made at six o'clock.

He liked breakfast by eight.

He liked dishes done by nine.

In Mr Merton's house, the clocks

buzzed

and rang

and beeped.

"No more clocks!" said Mrs Merton. "We are all going on a holiday. And we are not taking a clock or a watch with us!"

2

ROSTER
6 am Beds
8 am Breakfast
9 am Dishes

3

That night Mrs Merton packed her bag.

Beach ball
Sunglasses
Sun screen
Sun umbrella
Magazines
Books
Lemonade
Float board

Then she unpacked Mr Merton's bag.

She took out the clocks and the watches. "This is going to be a good holiday," she said.

Mr Merton did not like the beach. Sun umbrellas were out of line. Beach balls bounced out of time.

"I'll show everyone how to have a holiday!" he said. "This tent will be put up in five minutes! Get going!"

But when Mr Merton went to get his watches, they were not in his bag.

He looked through everything.
There were no watches.
There were no clocks.

"Who has taken my watches?" he said. "Who has taken my clocks?"

But no one heard. Mrs Merton and the children were swimming.

Mr Merton sat under a tree. He was grumpy. "What is the time?" he asked people. But no one was wearing a watch.

Then he saw the shadow of his tree. The shadow was moving across the sand. Mr Merton had an idea.

After lunch, he wrote "dishes" on the shadow.

When he felt tired, he wrote "sleep" on the shadow.

When the shadow was long and thin, he wrote "dinner" on the shadow.

9

Mr Merton's shadow clock
worked well.

And so did his family!

Mrs Merton cooked breakfast
by eight o'clock.

The children did the dishes
by nine.

"Our holiday is over,"
they wailed.

**But out to sea something
was happening . . .**

Out to sea, a large wave was rushing to the shore.

Sun umbrellas were packed up and picnic baskets were packed away. But Mr Merton stayed where he was. "Keep off my shadow clock!" he shouted at the sea.

But the wave

swish-swashed

onto the beach and over the shadow clock. It went over Mr Merton and sent him bobbing like a cork out to sea.

It sent him *splashing* and *swimming.*

It sent him leaping and laughing.

"What fun!" he said. And he

dived

over the waves.

"What fun it is to swim! Come in the water!" he shouted.

Mr Merton swam and swam.
He ate an ice cream for his
lunch and swam all afternoon.
He was so tired at night
he forgot to eat his dinner.

At the end of the week Mrs
Merton packed up the tent.
"We must go home," she said.

"But I don't want to go home,"
wailed Mr Merton. "I like the
beach. I'm having a good time.
I'm having a wonderful time!"

"Good!" said Mrs Merton, and
she smiled. "Holiday time is the
best time of all."

Narratives

What's a narrative?

A narrative is a story that has a plot (or storyline) with:

An introduction

A problem

A solution

How to Write a Narrative

Step One Write an introduction
An introduction tells the reader:

- Who the story is about (the characters)
- Where the story is set (the setting)
- When the story happened.

Step Two Write about the problem
Tell the reader about:

- The events of the story and the problems that the main characters meet
- What the characters <u>do</u> about the problem

I had to make a shadow clock so I could tell the time!

Step Three Write about the solution
Tell the reader how the problem is solved.

Don't forget!
A narrative can have more than one main character and other characters.

We are the main characters.

We are the other characters.

Guide Notes

Title: Mr Merton's Holiday
Stage: Launching Fluency

Text Form: Narrative
Approach: Guided Reading
Processes: Thinking Critically, Exploring Language, Processing Information
Written and Visual Focus: Illustrative Text, Roster, List, Scene Breaker

THINKING CRITICALLY

(sample questions)
- How do you know that this story is fiction?
- Why do you think Mr Merton liked things to be on time?
- Why do you think Mrs Merton said they were not taking a clock or a watch with them on holiday?
- Why do you think Mr Merton began to enjoy himself?
- What do you think will happen next time they go on holiday?

EXPLORING LANGUAGE

Terminology
Spread, author and illustrator credits, ISBN number

Vocabulary
Clarify: beeped, grumpy, swish-swashed, bobbing, wailed
Nouns: holiday, breakfast, clocks, tent, bag
Verbs: buzz, bounce, write, dive, swim
Singular/plural: dish/dishes, clock/clocks, holiday/holidays, ball/balls
Simile: bobbing like a cork

Print Conventions
Apostrophes – possessives (Mr Merton's holiday, Mr Merton's shadow clock), contraction (I'll)